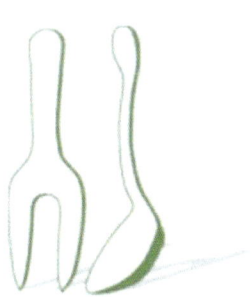

A FRESH START

FAMILY FRIENDLY HEALTHY RECIPES

HILLARY SHORT

*Dear Sam
Happy to meet a fellow chef!
Hillary*

First published in 2017, printed by CreateSpace

Copyright © 2017 by Hillary Short

All rights reserved. No part of this publication may be reproduced or distributed in any form or by any means, electronic or mechanical, or stored in a database or retrieval system without prior written permission from the author.

All rights reserved.
ISBN: 1543202373
ISBN-13: 978-1543202373

This book is for personal knowledge and entertainment purposes. The publisher and author is not responsible for any adverse effects arising directly or indirectly as a result of the information provided in the book.

Printed in the USA

Book Design by Jeff McDonald
Photography by Hillary Short and
Caroline Gray
www.carolinegrayphotography.com

DEDICATION

This year, whilst writing this book, I lost two important friends in my life. Lorna Kelly whose passion to help those less fortunate, and large charismatic personality, taught me to be a more spiritual person and to love myself unconditionally. Her wisdom and strength will always be a part of my psyche. My other loss was Iggy Hughes. A man who lived by his own rules, had a huge heart, large enough for everyone he met to feel special and loved. Unfortunately his large heart gave way too soon. His vibrant, generous, positive spirit is missed by so many people. Everyone we meet in our lives teaches us lessons. May I always carry a part of these two souls in my heart and carry on their legacies.

ACKNOWLEDGEMENTS

Thank you to all my family, clients and friends for urging me to write this book, and supporting me through the process. Foremost my Mother for being the person who passed on this passion for food and always supporting my adventurous spirit. Lelia Wood Smith for keeping a roof over my head. For chef Liz MacMaster for taking time to edit and read recipes for me, and to Liz Mortlock for the final edit. I couldn't have finished the project without all your help. And a special big thanks to Caroline Gray with www.carolinegrayphotography.com for providing some of the beautiful photography in my book.

CONTENTS

Introduction - 6

Kitchen Equipment - 8

Pantry Staples - 10

Vegan & Vegetarian - 11

Meat & Fish - 27

Sauces & Dressings - 48

Soups & Salads - 55

Grains, Nuts, Fermenting & Seeds - 66

Fridge Filling Instructions - 73

Bowl Dining - 75

Conclusion - 76

INTRODUCTION

My passion for healthy eating began 15 years ago when I needed to change my diet to lose weight and improve my health. At 40 years of age, I suffered from fatigue, achy joints, fibroids, and early hot flashes. On the advice of a nutritionist, I completely cut out sugar, wheat and dairy from my diet for an entire year. Soon, I was looking and feeling 10 years younger, and brimming with energy. Since then, my health has been excellent.

Working as a nanny for high profile families in London, New York and Los Angeles, I often ended up cooking the family meals, and as I wanted to stay in top shape myself, I prepared healthy meals for everybody. Usually, my clients were delighted, because they were, for the main, on permanent calorie-restricted diets.

This was the grilled-chicken-breast-and-salad crowd, so they enjoyed eating meals with reduced sugar, wheat & dairy (I now allowed myself to cook with a little of these). Once people sampled my delicious recipes, they didn't want to eat any other way. A few clients were initially hesitant to eat like this, but in a little while, they, too, became disciples. Soon I was being asked to cook for their dinner parties.

At that point, I made the transition to being a personal chef, opened the doors to a successful business named The Hungry Duchess, and after many years of cooking for the stars in Hollywood, I moved East, got certified as a health coach and started A Fresh Start. A company combining my cooking and health coaching skills. In my new working capacity, I often miss the days when I was cooking for a family in a large, open-plan kitchen, serene and centered, with a child to help me pull off the kale leaves from their stalks, whilst their older sibling pulls herbs and peels garlic cloves. From my experience with these little helpers, I know how much kids love to eat what they have helped produce.

They also eat well when they are hungry, so I recommend no snacks between meals and water as the only drink. I find that many families have plenty of fruit and vegetables in the fridge but when I open the pantry door, I see stacks of junky snacks! Throw them into the garbage! A hungry child will try the beet salad, and she may even like it! A diet filled with plenty of fresh fruits and vegetables produces happy, vibrant, healthy kids.

I find the latest generation of moms to be very health conscious. They are happy to feed their children plenty of fresh fruit and veggies. This book is inspired by them and intended for them – and for others who want to eat well and be well.

As a chef with many years' experience cooking delicious, healthy dishes for busy families, and as someone who keeps up with the latest food trends, I want to share my knowledge with others. I'm not a celebrity or a restaurateur: I'm a chef and certified health coach. My book is different from others because I cook for people on a daily basis, and these recipes have been tested time and again on many clients. I want to share my experience of changing eating habits and providing a "fresh start" to healthier eating choices.

This book will help you combine fresh ingredients—sometimes raw—to make meals that burst with natural flavors. Are you stuck in a routine? Are you still planning your meals around a hunk of meat? Is take-out pizza your meal default?

My recipes offer excellent and easy alternatives. You might even like to make a trendy "bowl" meal, which makes it easy to include super-foods and raw components in the same dish.

My book keeps things simple. As a go-to cookbook for whipping up dinner for family and friends, it includes only main dishes (except for one dessert I just had to share), because that is how families usually eat. No appetizers or desserts—at least not on weeknights— just delicious, wholesome, satisfying meals.

So turn the page and start cooking!

KITCHEN EQUIPMENT

I love stocking clients' kitchens with all the equipment needed to cook my recipes. Also working within all budgets. These are the utensils and appliance items I suggest any health conscious cook's kitchen will need. This list is will be useful for cooking my book's recipes.

VITAMIX The most important piece of equipment in a modern day kitchen. They are pricey, starting around $499. I buy them refurbished for less on either their website or on Amazon. For my recipes the least expensive model is fine. I love to make sauces, cauliflower rice, cashew cheese and smoothies in my Vitamix.

CHEF AND PARING KNIVES A great chef's knife is so important for any healthy conscious cook. Make sure you go to a reputable store, for example, Williams-Sonoma and buy a knife that feels right for you. I prefer the lighter weight Japanese knives. The only other knife I use is a paring knife, and maybe a bread knife. I never put my knives in the dishwasher and wipe them off rather than washing them.

WOODEN CHOPPING BOARD Good quality and buy the oil to condition your board regularly so it doesn't dry up and crack.

MINI CUISINART I can't live without mine. Great for quickly chopping small amounts of herbs, nuts, garlic etc.

SAUCEPANS The best and most expensive are copper, they are great heat conductors. For me they are too expensive and heavy. So many great brands out there to choose from, it all depends on your budget and preference

CROCKPOT Perfect for busy families needing to leave a stew or pulled meat slowly braising all day.

PYREX DISHES With plastic lids are ideal for storing food in the fridge, and they have roasting ones as well, also with lids. A necessary item for fridge fillings. I have a couple of sets in different shapes and sizes.

LEMON SQUEEZER And also something for squeezing limes and oranges. I use lots of citrus fruit in my dressings and sauces.

GARLIC PRESS

VEGETABLE PEELER

MICROPLANE For grating ginger or cheese. I prefer the long skinny one.

CAST IRON FRYING PAN Heavy but food tastes good and can go in the oven.

LE CREUSET DUTCH OVEN Pricey but so worth the investment for soups, curries etc.

PYREX MEASURING CUP Glass 2 cup size should be fine.

A GOOD SET OF MEASURING SPOONS

FINE MESH SIEVE So rice and lentils don't fall through the regular strainer.

A SET OF COOKING UTENSILS I like metal spatulas, wooden spoons, plastic for non stick pans if you still use them.

COOKING SCISSORS Not only for cutting meat but opening packets.

CAN OPENER

BAKING TRAYS For roasting, I prefer using a ceramic dish.

PANTRY STAPLES

I keep these items in stock so I can deviate from recipes. These staples are foods regularly used to cook with and I don't like being caught without them. Everyone's pantry items will look different, but these are my guidelines for a healthy supply of items.

Oils, Vinegars & Spices

Coconut Oil
Olive Oil
Avocado Oil
Sesame Oil
Safflower Oil
Grape Seed Oil
Red Wine Vinegar
Apple Cider Vinegar
Balsamic Vinegar
Cooking Wine
Sea Salt
Ground Pepper
Cumin
Turmeric
Cinnamon
Ground Coriander
Smoked Paprika
Nutmeg
Red Pepper Flakes

Perishable Fridge & Pantry Items

Butter
Red & Yellow Onions
Pasture-Raised Eggs
Ezekiel Bread
Almond Butter
Sugar Free Jam
Sauerkraut
Pickled Beets
Milk
Almond Milk
Coconut Milk
Sriracha
Vegenaise
Tamari
Fish Sauce
Garbanzo Beans
Black Beans
White Beans
Dijon Mustard
Tomato Paste
Diced Tins of Tomatoes
Thai Curry Paste

Assorted Nuts, Grains & Seeds

Tahini
Nutritional Yeast
Cans of Wild Salmon or Sardines
Gluten Free Crackers
Olives
Oranges
Lemons
Limes
Fresh Ginger
Garlic
Herbs

SWEETENERS

Local Raw Honey
Maple Syrup
Coconut Sugar

VEGAN & VEGETARIAN

When I first began cooking professionally I became passionate about creating vegan dishes. I love combining colors, textures and aromas. The creative process of handling, smelling and blending colors, smells and flavors, becomes even more pleasurable by playing loud music in the background, putting me in a great mood for the day. Give it a try in your kitchen. You won't be disappointed !!

Here are some of my favorite dishes in this category.

POACHED EGG ON TOAST WITH AVOCADO, RED ONION & PESTO

The inspiration for this breakfast dish comes from Kaffe K in Santa Monica. When I lived in Los Angeles I frequently popped in there for breakfast after a long, early morning hike in the Malibu mountains. This recipe is my favorite breakfast dish on their menu. It is absolutely divine, and contains lots of nutrients. Most of my recipes are for dinners, but I couldn't leave this one out. Here is my version of their dish.

- 2 slices tomato, thinly sliced
- 2 slices red onion, thinly sliced
- ¼ avocado, thinly sliced
- 2 eggs, poached to your satisfaction
- 2 slices of bread, toasted
- 1 tablespoon pesto (see my recipe)
- A drizzle of olive oil
- 1/8 teaspoon red pepper flakes
- Salt

HOW TO MAKE IT

Make toast and place on a plate, Add tomato slices, onion and avocado on top of the toast Gently place the poached egg on top and drizzle pesto over the top.

STUFFED PORTABELLO MUSHROOMS

A couple of new vegan cookbooks in particular caught my attention last year. The Plant Powered Way and The Undiet Cookbook. By checking out other chefs' recipes I am forced to keep up to date with my own repertoire of dishes. My favorite discoveries were about bowls and stuffing a mushroom or sweet potato with lots of nutritionally tasty veggies, nuts and sprouts. These dishes are great because I can easily blend together the flavors of cooked and raw foods. Not only are raw foods nutritious but they add extra flavor to the dish.

- 4-6 large portobello mushrooms (1 mushroom per person)
- 2 sweet potatoes
- 12 brussels sprouts thinly sliced
- 1 shallot thinly sliced
- Coconut oil spray
- 1 teaspoon olive oil
- 1/4 cup sprouted mung beans cooked
- Salt & pepper

For toppings, I suggest my tahini dressing recipe, a handful of my grated nuts, nutritional yeast and garlic topping recipe, and a handful of fresh herbs of your choice

HOW TO MAKE IT

Bake sweet potatoes for 40 mins, until soft, at 350°F. Remove skins once the potato has cooled down, and mash them with a fork. Sautée Brussels sprouts and shallot in a frying pan on medium heat, with salt and pepper until soft and mushy – about 10 minutes. Spray portobello mushrooms with coconut oil and salt, place cap side up in a roasting pan with 1 cup of water and bake for 10 minutes at 325°F. Remove mushrooms from oven and turn them over ready for stuffing. Place mashed sweet potato into each mushroom's cavity, sprinkle with the cooked sprouted mung beans. Add a spoonful of Brussels sprout mixture. Place the stuffed mushrooms bake in the oven and bake at 350°F for 15 minutes. Remove from oven and put each mushroom on a serving plate, don't worry about the overspill, this dish looks messy. Add dressing, nut topping and herbs. Serve with a salad or a bunch of arugula. This dish looks messy but is delicious. The first time you make this dish it may feel arduous because of all the different ingredients, but once you have made it once or twice it becomes simpler. I find kids love this dish, the bursting colors and flavors are fun to play with.

The portobello mushroom could be replaced by a sweet potato stuffed with similar toppings.

MEXICAN BLACK BEAN BURGERS

A favorite dish for my vegetarian clients, but I also discovered my meat eating friends and clients also love this recipe because they are so tasty and nutritious. A dish that parents can get their kids to eat as well. This recipe is stolen from the Fine Cooking magazine, I slightly adapt them for simplification and flavor.

- **1 15oz can black beans**
- **3 scallions thinly sliced**
- **1 garlic clove finely chopped**
- **½ cup cilantro finely chopped**
- **½ cup breadcrumbs**
- **1 egg**
- **1 teaspoon chili powder**
- **1 teaspoon cumin powder**
- **Salt**
- **3 tablespoons grape seed oil**

HOW TO MAKE IT

Strain and rinse the black beans. Mash them with a potato masher. Add the remainder of the ingredients to the bowl and mix with your hands. Refrigerate mixture for ½ hour before frying. Form 4-6 bean burgers with your hands. Warm a frying pan, add salt and grape seed oil, gently warm the oil on medium. Add burgers to the pan. Cook for 5 minutes, turn the burgers and heat for another 5 minutes on medium heat. Turn down the heat to low, cover the pan and heat for 5 more minutes to cook through Serve with my vegan sauce or my guacamole sauce, and maybe a salad.

NOODLES, EGGPLANT, TOFU, RED ONION & MANGO

I adapted this recipe from an Ottolenghi cookbook. His recipes are amongst my favorites. During the early Hungry Duchess days, Ottolgenghi was one of my mentors because his cookbooks help me to be a more creative, modern, healthier chef. His recipes tend to be arduous due to the use of so many ingredients, so I slightly adapt most of them. A great trick I use for the extra firm tofu, to firm it up even more, place tofu on a plate, add a plate on top of it and a can for weighting it down. Leave tofu for ½ hour to get more liquid out of the tofu, this makes it really firm.

Dressing:
1/2 cup rice vinegar
1 tablespoon honey
1/2 teaspoon salt
2 garlic cloves peeled and crushed
1 teaspoon sriracha
1 teaspoon sesame oil
1 lime's juice

Ingredients:
8oz extra firm tofu cut into 1" cubes
2 eggplants diced
8oz soba noodles
1 mango finely chopped
1 cup fresh basil finely chopped
2 cups fresh cilantro finely chopped

HOW TO MAKE IT

Add tofu and eggplant to a roasting pan in 1 layer, add salt and olive oil, bake at 350°F for 30 minutes until browned. Slightly warm all the dressing ingredients in saucepan, to melt the honey. Boil noodles as directed on the package. Remove and drain water. In a large serving bowl add all the ingredients. Adding the dressing once ready to serve. This dish is perfect served at room temperature.

SIMON RIMMER'S BANANA DAHL RECIPE

A friend gave me Rimmer's vegetarian cookbook The Accidental Vegetarian. I was pleasantly surprised by his recipes, they are unfussy and turn favorite recipes into vegetarian dishes. This Dahl recipe is recipe is one of my favorites. The sweet, flavorful addition of bananas give the dish a unique flavor. Some clients find the banana addition strange, but the dish tastes equally good without them.

1 tablespoon grape seed oil
1 onion peeled and sliced
2 garlic cloves peeled and finely chopped
1" ginger cubed and grated
a pinch ground turmeric
8oz dried red lentils
16oz vegetable stock
Salt and pepper
1 teaspoon ground cumin
1 teaspoon ground coriander
1 teaspoon garam masala
4 firm bananas peeled and sliced*
2 tablespoons chopped cilantro leaves

HOW TO MAKE IT

Warm oil in saucepan, add onions, garlic and ginger. Sautée for 8-10 minutes until soft. Add turmeric and red lentils, and stir for 2 minutes. Add stock, bring to the boil then simmer, uncovered for 15 minutes. Add salt, pepper, spices and simmer for 10 more minutes. Add the bananas for the last 2 minutes.

Serve with a cilantro garnish

GREEN BEANS WITH ORANGE AND HAZELNUTS

Another one of my favorite dishes from an Ottolenghi cookbook. I have simplified his recipe for a family dinner or dinner party side dish. Very popular, giving a slight twist and added flavor to green beans.

1 pound french green beans
1 garlic clove finely chopped
3/4 cup hazelnuts
Bunch chives finely chopped
1 orange rind grated and juice squeezed
1 tablespoon grape seed oil

HOW TO MAKE IT

Boil green beans for 3 minutes. Drain the water and add to serving bowl. Brown hazelnuts in frying pan. Remove from heat and rub in towel to remove most of the skins. Then pound the towel with a jar to lightly smash the hazelnuts, or coarsely cut them in the towel with a knife. Add all the remaining ingredients to the beans and serve at room temperature. A simple and delicious side dish.

HOMEMADE COLESLAW

I have always made my coleslaw this way. Something I learned from my mother. Much more flavor than cabbage mixed with mayonnaise. I love the taste of kale or cabbage chiffonade, the technique of thinly slicing lengthwise. For a quick lesson to this method, google cabbage chiffonade on YouTube and there are several great videos

1/2 white cabbage chiffonade
1/4 red onion finely sliced
Salt

Dressing:
1/4 cup grape seed oil
1/4 cup red wine vinegar
1 teaspoon Dijon mustard
1 garlic clove crushed
1/8 teaspoon honey

HOW TO MAKE IT

Put cabbage and red onion in bowl. Sprinkle salt on top and leave to blend whilst you make the dressing. Whisk dressing ingredients together, then mix with the cabbage and stir. Leave at room temperature for 1/2 hour to soften, then put into refrigerator until needed.

Keeps up to 3 days.

CAULIFLOWER RICE

Cauliflower rice is one of the latest food fads. Not only is it a nice replacement for carbs, but it has a nice flavor and is highly nutritious. I have repeatedly fussed with finding the perfect recipe, and finally realized it best to be kept simple. Also, the mini Cuisinart seems to provide the best texture for me, I tend to over mush cauliflower in the Vitamix.

1 cauliflower cut into small florets
Pinch of saffron or turmeric
Pinch of salt
1 tablespoon olive oil

HOW TO MAKE IT

Cut the cauliflower into little florets and make the white stalks small. Add about a handful of cauliflower at a time to the Vitamix or mini Cuisinart and chop on low. Take out when the cauliflower has a rice texture to it, and put in a bowl. Repeat until all of the cauliflower is finely grated. Add cauliflower to a frying pan with olive oil and salt, gently sautee for about 5 minutes. Add turmeric or saffron after a couple of minutes. It is that simple, especially now that everywhere is selling cauliflower already 'riced' for you. A popular replacement for carbs.

MEAT & FISH DISHES

Although I prefer creating vegetable dishes, I love eating meat and fish. My attempt at being a vegan lasted 4 months. My tiredness and passing of gas was problematic. As a firm believer that everybody's needs are different in regards to diet, it is best people follow their own intuition about what works best for them. Saying this though, I believe that by limiting our sugar intake keeps us all healthier. In my personal experience, my energy levels and joints are at their optimum when I cut out sugar, wheat and dairy from my diet. However, when I cut out meat and fish from my diet I end up eating too many carbs. For me, protein curbs sugar cravings. Everybody has a different body type, but this eating style works best for me.

THAI CURRY RECIPE

This simple, adaptable recipe is a firm favorite with clients and friends. Spices, herbs and coconut milk is always a winning combination for both nutrition and flavor.

- **1-2 tablespoons green Thai curry paste (spice taste)**
- 1 can coconut milk
- 1 small can coconut cream unsweetened
- 1 pound shrimp raw, deveined & skinless or
- 1 pound boneless, skinless chicken breasts cubed
- 1 red pepper thinly sliced lengthwise
- **Handful snap peas**
- 1 tablespoon fish sauce
- **Handful fresh basil finely chopped**
- 1 fresh lime's juice
- 1 tablespoon maple syrup
- **Salt and pepper**

HOW TO MAKE IT

Add coconut milk, coconut cream and curry paste to a large frying pan. Stir and simmer for 5 minutes. Add all the veggies, except the basil and simmer for 7 minutes until softened. Add the shrimp or chicken and simmer until cooked through. Add basil, simmer for 2 minutes and serve.

I love this curry served with black rice.

GREEK ROAST LAMB

We all love the fresh Mediterranean flavors of a Greek style dinner. So fresh tasting with many flavors combined together. The salad and tzatziki that compliments this dish are featured in their relevant chapters.

¼ cup olive oil
Salt and pepper
3 garlic cloves crushed
½ tablespoon of rosemary
4 ½ pound leg of lamb

HOW TO MAKE IT

Add all the ingredients, except the lamb, to your mini Cuisinart and blend together. Place lamb on a rack in a roasting pan (if you have a roasting pan with a rack), then rub the mixture onto the lamb using your hands. Leave the joint out on the counter for ½ hour to marinade. Then roast in the middle of the oven at 375°F for 2 hours. Let the meat rest on a cutting board, covered with aluminum foil for 20 minutes before cutting the meat.

TACOS

A firm favorite with children and adults. There are plenty of ways to make this Mexican staple. But this method is most popular to my clients, and is healthy, nutritious and tasty.

1 ½ pound ground beef

Mixed spices for flavor:

1 teaspoon salt
1 teaspoon chili powder
1/2 teaspoon ground cumin
1/4 teaspoon red pepper flakes
1/8 teaspoon cayenne pepper
1/4 teaspoon garlic powder
1/4 teaspoon dried oregano
1 tablespoon white wine vinegar
1 cup water

Side fixings:

1 14oz can black or pinto beans
1 iceberg lettuce thinly sliced
Chopped cilantro
1/2 diced red onion
1 cup cucumber diced
1 large tomato diced
1 avocado diced
Grated cheese Mexican blend
1 cup plain greek yoghurt
Serve with hard shell corn tacos

HOW TO MAKE IT

Add ground beef to a frying pan with all the blended spices. Simmer for 20 minutes. Whilst the meat is simmering prepare all the sides into bowls on the table. Warm the taco shells. Place the meat in a bowl on the table and serve family style. Absolute family favorite.

SALMON SALSA VERDE

I adapted this meal from a Rick Stein recipe. The dish is the most popular meal I offer. That is why I photographed the raw ingredients for the book's cover. I love the different colors, shapes and flavors that the raw, unprepared recipe represents. It is tasty, nutritious and family friendly. Once you have made it a couple of times, it is also pretty easy.

- Large handful flat leaf parsley
- Small handful mint
- ½ tablespoon Dijon mustard
- 1 tablespoon capers
- 3 anchovies
- 2 garlic cloves
- ½ lemon juice
- 1 teaspoon of olive oil

Bash all the ingredients together in mortar and pestle. Or chop in a mini Cuisinart

- 2 pounds skinless salmon cut into 2 pieces.
- ¼ teaspoon red pepper flakes
- 1 tablespoon capers
- Fresh thyme sprigs
- Olive oil
- 10 tablespoons water
- 4 tomatoes thinly sliced
- 2 garlic cloves peeled and sliced
- 1 tablespoon olive oil

HOW TO MAKE IT

Place tomatoes layered in baking dish. Add water, olive oil, chili flakes, capers, thyme, salt and pepper. Place 1 piece of salmon on top of the tomato mix. Add the pounded herb mixture to the top of the fish. Place second piece of salmon on top of the other piece of salmon. Add salt, a few more chili flakes, a glug of olive oil and 3 thyme stalks. Bake in the oven at 375°F for 30 minutes covered, then 15 minutes uncovered.

I serve this dish with roast potatoes and green beans, sometimes adding a French dressing to the warm beans.

FLANK STEAK WITH MARINADE

The flank steak is a reasonably priced cut of beef. When cut thinly against the grain and marinated with this Asian flavor, it has proven to be very popular and an easy dish.

Marinade:
2 garlic cloves crushed
1" ginger grated
2 tablespoons rice vinegar
2 tablespoons lime juice
¼ cup tamari
2 tablespoons sesame oil
1 teaspoon Asian chili sauce
¼ cup grape seed oil
½ tablespoon honey
1 whole flank steak – around 1 ½ pounds

HOW TO MAKE IT

Marinate the flank steak with all the marinade ingredients, place in refrigerator for 2-4 hours, or at room temperature for an hour. Remove flank steak from marinade and pat dry. Keep the remaining marinade and warm gently in a saucepan. If using the marinade after it has been sitting on raw meat makes you queasy, before adding the marinade to the steak leave some of the sauce out for warming instead of using it all for the marinade. I grill or bake my flank steak, If grilling, on a high grill, sear on both sides. Then turn down the grill to medium, close the lid and cook for 4 minutes on each side. Remove steak and let sit for 5 minutes. Finely slice against the grain.

To bake the steak instead, place steak in a roasting pan and bake uncovered at 350°F for 30 minutes. The steak can be served as part of a bowl meal, as the protein component, or with vegetables and a starch. So great for family dinners.

BAKED COD WITH PINE NUT & ANCHOVY SALSA

This fish dish is similar to the salmon salsa verde. The combination is deliciously nutritious. As cod is mild tasting and inexpensive, it is great for feeding larger families. For a fancier fish choice for a dinner party, I suggest halibut.

Salsa Ingredients:
A bunch Italian parsley, finely chopped
3 anchovies in olive oil finely chopped
Packet chives finely chopped
1 lemon juice and grated rind
1 small shallot finely diced
4 tablespoons pine nuts
½ cup olive oil
2 pounds cod fillet

HOW TO MAKE IT

Mix the salsa ingredients together. Or if the chopping is too arduous, place all the salsa ingredients in your mini Cuisinart (except the pine nuts, stir them in after chopping) and let that magical device take care of the chopping for you. Place the cod in a roasting pan. Spread the salsa mixture over the fish. Cover and bake at 350°F for 25 minutes.

THAI STYLE CRAB CAKES

I seldom cook with crab but decided to try this Gwyneth Paltrow recipe for something different. They are a huge hit and are lighter and healthier than your traditional stodgy ones.

- **1 pound crabmeat (buy the canned, refrigerated brand)**
- 1 tablespoon finely chopped mint leaves
- 1 tablespoon finely chopped cilantro
- 2 tablespoons vegenaise
- 3 finely chopped scallions
- 1 egg
- 1 tablespoon tamari
- 1 teaspoon red pepper flakes
- 1 teaspoon lime juice
- 1/2 cup Panko
- grape seed oil

HOW TO MAKE IT

Mix all the ingredients together with your hands. Mold into 4 patties. Cover and refrigerate for at least 1 hour, but no more than 12 hours. Heat oil medium high in a skillet. Place the 4 patties into pan, heat for 5 minutes, turn and heat for another 5 minutes. Cover the pan and turn down to low for 3 minutes and serve.

I love eating these crab cakes with my tartare sauce recipe. Accompany them with a salad and a green veggie. There is no need to add a starch because of the Panko.

MY FAVORITE FISH PAELLA DISH

I discovered this recipe in the Los Angeles Times and have been making it for many years. A firm favorite with everyone I make it for. Grating the tomatoes takes practice. I buy large ripe tomatoes, about 2 or 3, cut them in half and grate them into a bowl. Using the large grating option. It takes a bit of time to do, but the process is well worth the end result.

- 5 tablespoons olive oil
- 1/2 cup finely chopped onion
- 1/4 cup finely chopped garlic
- 1 cup grated tomato pulp
- ¾ pound cod fillet cut into bite size cubes
- 8 squid bodies cut into ring
- 1/4 cup dry white wine
- 2 1/2 cups fish or vegetable broth
- Pinch of saffron
- 1 bay leaf
- 1 tablespoon salt
- 1 1/2 cup rice
- 8 large deveined and peeled shrimp
- 8 fresh mussels
- 12" paella pan

HOW TO MAKE IT

Make the soffrito: Heat pan to medium high. Add 3 tablespoons of oil, heat and add onions and garlic. Sautée for 5 minutes until soft. Add tomato pulp and cook for 10 minutes until reduced to a 1/4 of the original amount. Remove from pan and place the soffrito in a bowl. Add the remaining oil to pan. Heat the oil and then add cod and squid, sear on medium high for 2 minutes, reduce heat to medium and add wine, stir and reduce for about 2 minutes. Add the soffrito, vegetable broth, bay leaf, salt and saffron to the fish. The add the rice, spreading evenly around the pan. Make sure rice is immersed in the liquid, do not stir. Boil then simmer. Arrange mussels and shrimp on top and simmer for 15 minutes. Remove from heat, cover with paper towels and let sit for 5 minutes before serving. Can be left at room temperature for up to 2 hours.

I have also made this dish using cauliflower rice instead of regular rice.

MY FAVORITE CHICKEN CURRY

Indian curry is my favorite food. We grew up eating lots of curry because my mother is colonial British. She was raised in Kenya where there was a huge Indian influence in the 1950's. This is my favorite curry recipe, I bought a coffee grinder just for grinding these spices together. This recipe can be finicky with all the blending and grinding, but after a while you get used to it and it feels less arduous. Sometimes to save time, I use powdered spices so that I don't need to grind. Here is my adaptation of a Madhur Jaffrey recipe, she is my favorite Indian cook.

Spices for grinding together:
- 2 teaspoon cumin seeds
- 1 teaspoon black peppercorns
- 1 teaspoon cardamom seeds
- 1 cinnamon stick
- 1/2 teaspoon black mustard seeds
- 5 tablespoons white wine vinegar
- 1 teaspoon salt
- 1/4 teaspoon cayenne pepper
- 1 tablespoon honey
- 3 tablespoons coconut oil

- 2 yellow onions finely chopped
- 6 tablespoons water
- 1" cube of ginger
- 10 garlic cloves peeled
- 1 tablespoon coriander seeds
- 1/2 teaspoon ground turmeric
- 2 pounds boneless, skinless chicken breast Cut up into 1" cubes
- 8oz tomato sauce
- 1 14oz tin coconut cream or milk

HOW TO MAKE IT

Grind the 5 spices into a powder. Fry onions with 5 tablespoons of oil until slightly brown in a large saucepan. Blend the ground spices with the vinegar, cayenne pepper, salt and honey. Add to brown onions, and simmer for 1 minute together. Blend garlic and ginger with 3 tablespoons of water into paste. Add to onions, simmer for 2 minutes and add turmeric and coriander. Add chicken to mixture and brown the chicken. Add tomato sauce and coconut cream. Cover saucepan and bake in the oven at 300°F for 2 hours.

I serve the chicken curry with basmati rice or cauliflower rice, and mango chutney.

MY NAUGHTY BBQ CHICKEN

This recipe does contain sugar in the tomato ketchup, hence the naughty chicken title, but as everyone loves this easy to make chicken dish, I couldn't leave it out of my book.

Dry rub:
1 teaspoon paprika
1 teaspoon cumin
½ teaspoon garlic powder
Salt & pepper to taste

Sauce mix:
1 cup ketchup
1 garlic clove crushed
1 tablespoon olive oil
3 tablespoons honey
1 tablespoon Dijon mustard
1 tablespoon Apple cider vinegar
2 tablespoons Worcestershire sauce

6 chicken thighs with skin and bone in or skin on chicken breasts

HOW TO MAKE IT

Mix the dry mix together in a bowl and add chicken thighs or breasts. Blend well. Heat the oil in an oven proof frying pan and add the chicken to the pan, sautee until browned on both sides. Whilst chicken is browning mix all the sauce ingredients together, once chicken is brown add the sauce mix, to the pan, stir and cover the pan, and place in the oven at 350°F for 40 minutes.

I serve this with cauliflower rice and my home made coleslaw.

SAUCES & DRESSINGS

I love making my own sauces and dressings. This is where I feel at my best creatively. Everyone absolutely loves my sauces. I keep ingredients simple, fresh and nutritious, and work primarily with my mini cuisinart. My cooking philosophy is to cook with fine quality, fresh ingredients and add simple sauces and dressings. I love fresh herbs, garlic, ginger and spices. Also, by adding a good quality oil you enhance the flavors.

TAHINI DRESSING

I mostly use this versatile dressing in my bowls, but this dressing can be used to accompany so many different meals. Tahini, which is crushed sesame seeds, is a nutritious super food. Although high in fat their nutritional value is so worth the extra calories. It goes without saying how deliciously tasty this is. Tahini is a great substitute for creamy dressings.

- 1/4 cup tahini
- 1/2 cup water
- 1 orange, lime or lemon juice
- 1 tablespoon toasted sesame oil
- 1 teaspoon ginger peeled
- 1 garlic clove peeled
- 1 teaspoon maple syrup
- Small handful of fresh cilantro, flat leaf parsley or mint. Or a mix of all.
- 1/8 teaspoon Asian chili paste

HOW TO MAKE IT

Add all the ingredients to the mini cuisinart or blender and thoroughly mix. Adjust the amount of water depending on what you will be using the dressing for.

MANGO LIME VINAIGRETTE

My clients either love or hate this dressing because it is very sweet and tangy. I love it, for it's unique flavor and how it compliments the Mecca Azteca Salad. Both the salad and the dressing are slightly adapted from the Native Foods Cafe menu and their cookbook.

- 1/2 cup frozen mango
- 1/2 cup safflower or sunflower oil
- 1/8 cup maple syrup
- 1/4 cup lime juice
- 1 tablespoon rice vinegar
- 1 teaspoon salt
- 1 teaspoon fresh ginger

HOW TO MAKE IT

Add to mini Cuisinart or blender and lightly dress salads.

A SIMPLE TRADITIONAL FRENCH DRESSING

I use this dressing to add to coleslaw, or a grated fennel or grated carrot and red onion salad. Although for plain salads I generally serve a big bowl of spring mix or arugula with my nut topping and a good quality olive oil and balsamic vinegar.

- 1 finely minced garlic clove
- 1 teaspoon Dijon mustard
- 2 tablespoons red wine vinegar
- 1/8 teaspoon honey
- 6 tablespoons grape seed oil

HOW TO MAKE IT

Add all the ingredients to a bowl and then gently whisk in the grape seed oil. The dressing is that simple and bursts with goodness and flavor

BASIC ASIAN STYLE VINAIGRETTE

Asian salads are extremely popular with my healthy diners. This dressing is perfect when you are eating an Asian inspired meal. Kids love the salty / sweet combination to disguise the greens flavors. A great way to get kids to eat greens.

- 1 tablespoon fresh ginger grated
- 2 teaspoons minced garlic
- 1/4 cup finely chopped cilantro
- 1/4 cup rice vinegar
- 1/8 cup tamari
- 2 tablespoons fresh lime juice
- 1 1/2 teaspoons honey
- 1 teaspoon Asian chili paste

HOW TO MAKE IT

Whisk all the above ingredients together and slowly whisk in:

- 1 tablespoon sesame oil toasted
- 1/2 cup safflower oil.

SIMPLE, ADAPTABLE PESTO

Everybody loves a good pesto. Each time I adapt my pesto recipe I enjoy it even more. However for caloric reasons I tend to eat more salsa verde or chimichurri these days. But who can resist a tasty pesto in the summer time. If you order a weekly CSA farm box throughout the summer months, which financially supports local farms, and enables you to eat more fresh and local produce; after a few weeks of boxes you will be bored of eating the piles of greens landing on your doorstep every week. Last summer I discovered how to create plenty of tasty greens to freeze by using them up with the other ingredients in this recipe. Then you have a nutritious, raw, dressing or sauce. The pesto is simple to freeze for the winter months. To make this as a dressing I add some water to thin down the pesto.

This is my basic vegan recipe, I prefer the taste of nutritional yeast instead of parmesan cheese. Also, If you are allergic to walnuts, use different nuts, including the classic pine nuts. Different greens and herbs can replace basil, or even blend up the tops of carrots and beets. Relax and have fun producing "pesto'd" greens !! I can't emphasize enough the nutritional value of eating raw foods. A word of caution however, for my readers new to the flavor of nutritional yeast, it has a strong taste, so apply sparingly at first. There are many brands of nutritional yeast, depends on what supermarket you shop at.

3 cups basil
2 garlic cloves
1 tablespoon lemon juice
½ teaspoon Salt
1 tablespoon nutritional yeast

HOW TO MAKE IT

Blend everything but the nutritional yeast together in blender and slowly drizzle and blend 1/2 cup high quality olive oil. Stir in the nutritional yeast.

CHIMICHURRI

I love chimichurri, an Argentinian favorite for meats and fish dishes. It is tasty, fresh, and simple

HOW TO MAKE IT

Add to mini cuisinart or blender:
1/2 cup parsley
1/4 cup cilantro
Handful of mint
3 tablespoons red wine vinegar
1 tablespoon fresh lemon juice
4 garlic gloves
Blend, then remove to bowl

Whisk in:
1 teaspoon crushed pepper flakes
½ cup olive oil
1 tablespoon fresh lemon juice
Salt and pepper to preferred taste

TZATZIKI

I don't often use or eat dairy , but I love my tzatziki recipe as an accompaniment for my roast lamb and greek salad. This sauce really needed to be included in the book.

16oz Greek yoghurt (2% fat)
1 English cucumber grated into a sieve
1 teaspoon fresh lemon juice
2 finely minced garlic cloves
Salt and pepper

HOW TO MAKE IT

Lightly salt the grated cucumber and leave in the sink draining for 1/2 hour
Stir together the remainder of the ingredients into a bowl. Add the cucumber and mix everything together. Add salt & pepper to your personal taste.

SALSA & AVOCADOS

I am not a salsa lover, too mushy for my palate. But I love finely dicing the following ingredients and serving them in individual bowls at the table. Perfect additions for salads and taco toppings. I usually have these items in my pantry so I can throw them together as a last minute accompaniment to my dishes.

Avocado
Cilantro
Slices of lime for squeezing
Red onion finely diced

I always have at least 4 avocados in the pantry. I also love this green goddess salad dressing on chiffonaded kale or arugula.

1 avocado
2 garlic cloves
½ fresh lemon juice
¼ cup cilantro
½ teaspoon sriracha
¼ cup olive oil

HOW TO MAKE IT

Blend all the ingredients together in a mini Cuisinart or blender.

Are you starting to notice my favorite ingredients for cooking? Also, where I use lemon juice as an ingredient for a dish, you can substitute with fresh lime or orange juice. Same with my herb choices, for example, try flat leaf parsley instead of cilantro, also, by adding a bit of fresh mint to a sauce, it freshens up any of my dressings, gives it a bit of a zing!! With practice you will find chopping and changing herbs and citruses will become second nature. Also explore different vinegars. I love rice wine, sherry, apple cider and red wine vinegars.

SALADS

My salads are combined together to compliment each other. I think of salad as an orchestra. The combining of the ingredients enhances your taste buds. Living in Los Angeles meant experimenting with lots of salads for the right flavors. I needed to get to work and come up with some interesting, diverse choices. My salads became fun to make and fast became favorites. Now that I am a health coach I incorporate salads into my diet because the raw ingredients are a nutritionally valuable meal choice, to accompany cooked food. I hope you enjoy these combinations as much as I do. They may seem arduous at first – with all the necessary chopping of several ingredients, but I promise you all the effort you put in will pay off tenfold.

CHOPPED MEXICAN SALAD

When I began my Hungry Duchess business I needed to build a varied selection of recipes to offer clients. I had to do plenty of research into fresh and tasty recipes that were modern and family friendly. A fellow foodie, Leslie Shaffer, bought me a year's subscription to Fine Cooking magazine. This really useful gift brought me so many amazing, fresh, easy, modern flavored recipes. For example this chopped Mexican salad recipe is adapted from the magazine. I love the ingredient and dressing combination, and is a firm favorite for friends and clients. Although the prep work takes time because of all the chopping, it gets easier after making the recipe a couple of times.

Honey-lime-cumin vinaigrette:
1 garlic clove crushed
1/2 teaspoon salt
3 tablespoons fresh lime juice
3 tablespoons fresh orange juice
2 teaspoons finely chopped shallot
1 tablespoon honey
3/4 teaspoon cumin seed toasted in pan and ground
1/4 cup olive oil
Ground pepper

For pepper and corn:
2 red bell peppers diced
1/2 bag of frozen corn
1 tablespoon olive oil
Salt and pepper - a light sprinkle

Other ingredients for the salad's assembling:
2 large firm tomatoes cored and seeded into 1/4" dice
1 small jicama peeled and cut into 1/4" dice
2 avocados 1/4" dice
1 15oz can black beans drained and rinsed
1/4 cup coarsley chopped cilantro

HOW TO MAKE IT

Roast the corn, peppers, salt and oil in oven at 425°F for 20 minutes. Leave to cool. Make the vinaigrette dressing by whisking all the ingredients together in a bowl. To assemble the salad: place all the salad ingredient onto a platter and sprinkle with cilantro. Keep each item separated so people can serve themselves and mix their own ingredients together. Have the dressing on the side so people can add dressing to their salad once on their individual plate. The ingredients can be fully prepared as above onto a large serving platter, covered and refrigerated for up to 4 hours.

MECCA AZTECA SALAD

Yes, more chopping required. But all this chopping pays off, I promise you. This salad compliments the Mango Lime Vinaigrette dressing. This recipe is adapted from The Native Foods cookbook. If you like fruity, tangy, sweet salads and dressings, this will become a firm favorite, this combination of ingredients just burst in your mouth.

- 1 cup tomatoes chopped
- 1 cup cucumber chopped
- 1 cup jicama peeled and chopped
- 1 cup red onion chopped
- 2 tablespoons fresh squeezed lemon juice
- 2 teaspoons salt
- 2 cups mixed salad greens
- 4 cups quinoa cooked

Topping:
- 2 cups fresh cilantro leaves
- 4 tablespoons roasted pumpkin seeds (I sautée them gently in a frying pan, until brown)
- 1/8 teaspoon cayenne pepper

Mix these 3 items together for a topping

1 cup of mango lime vinaigrette
(see recipe in the sauces and dressing chapter)

HOW TO MAKE IT

Assemble: add salad leaves to plates. Put the chopped veggies on top of the lettuce leaves. Add some dressing. Then sprinkle with the topping.

THE HUNGRY DUCHESS' CHOPPED SALAD

My fridge filling clientele love me to chop up and leave a salad for them to eat for the next few days. This is how I assemble this. I heavily rely upon items at the olive bar in Whole Foods.

1 container Arugula (or another leaf if desired)
Container cherry tomatoes halved
2 Persian cucumbers diced
1 orange peeled and thinly sliced from segments
4" block feta cheese cut into ¼" cubes
1/4 red onion peeled and diced
10 pitted olives
Handful nuts toasted

HOW TO MAKE IT

To assemble. place lettuce in a large salad bowl, each ingredient is individually placed into a small container and then sits on top of the lettuce in their containers. Cover the large bowl of all the ingredients and refrigerate. Serve as required. I like a good quality balsamic vinegar and olive oil served with this salad. But this salad is also tasty with any of my dressings.

To warm up this salad on my plate, I sometimes add some warm rice mixed in with the ingredients.

GREEK SALAD

I love a good, fresh, simple, Greek salad. Especially on a hot day with lamb. Simple, clean, Mediterranean dining. It is just about the ingredients. Enjoy my interpretation of this favorite.

1 packet of 3 romaine lettuces thinly sliced
15 cherry tomatoes halved
1/2 English cucumber diced
12 pitted black olives
5oz feta cheese diced
1/4 red onion peeled and diced
Fresh mint handful thinly chopped
1 tablespoon oregano dried

Dressing:
¼ cup olive oil
1/8 cup red wine vinegar
1 garlic peeled and crushed
Salt and pepper

HOW TO MAKE IT

Mix all the salad ingredients in a bowl. Toss the salad with dressing just before serving.

KALE SALAD

I went through a phase of making & eating kale salad every day. It is a highly nutritious super food. This recipe is my preferred method for eating raw kale, otherwise the leaves are too tough for me.

- 1 bunch Lacinato kale
- 1 tablespoon olive oil
- 2 garlic cloves crushed
- 1 orange juiced
- A handful of seeds & nuts
- 1 avocado peeled and diced

HOW TO MAKE IT

Strip the kale leaves from the tough stalks using your hands. Then bunch a handful of leaves at a time and chiffonade them. Add olive oil and massage the leaves with your hands until softened slightly. Mix in the rest of the ingredients and serve immediately. If serving later, massage the leaves with ½ the amount of olive oil and leave in the fridge. Add the rest of the ingredients before serving.

There are many variations to try with oiled, massaged, kale leaves. Any type of finely chopped nuts, adding diced tomatoes, adding warm grains to eat the salad warm, adding nutritional yeast to give a cheesy flavor etc. Endless possibilities. I will be adding a video onto my Facebook page showing my readers how to chiffon kale.

Facebook page is: www.facebook.com/healthcoachhillaryshort/

GRAINS, NUTS, FERMENTING & SEEDS

Grains

I rarely eat sugar, wheat or dairy. If I decide to eat or cook with grains I generally cook with gluten free options. Grains are high in nutritional value, and are a nice addition to a family meal. As I am a novice to grain cooking my book doesn't have any grain recipes, but I urge you to experiment with cooking grains. These are some gluten free options to pick up and try – quinoa, rice, millet, amaranth, teff, buckwheat and sorghum. Email me with some nice ideas. I do make quinoa into tabouli, which is tasty and disguises the taste of quinoa. Because quinoa is considered a protein, the grain is considered a good carb free option.

Legumes

I love beans and several of my recipes use them. For the busy home cook, I suggest using cans of beans, but I always use dried lentils. Be brave and try all the various colors of lentils. And try cooking your lentils blended in with rice. It gives the rice and lentils a deeper flavor. The beans I mostly use are black beans, white beans, chickpeas and black-eyed peas. Try black-eyed peas blended in with sautéed, garlic flavored collard greens, absolutely delicious side dish.

Nuts & Seeds

Nuts and seeds are such a great nutritional addition to a meal, especially as a salad topping, and a great addition for vegan meals. Nuts are great as a substitute for dairy. I drink almond milk in my tea instead of dairy. I don't miss the dairy at all. My favorite brand is unsweetened Califa. The nuts and seeds I love sprinkling on my food, or using in recipes, are almonds, walnuts, cashews, hazelnuts, pistachio, hemp, flax, chia, sesame or pumpkin. I generally lightly toast my seeds or nuts in a small frying pan, on a medium to low heat for a couple of minutes, this adds a toastier flavor to the dish.

Sprouting

Sprouted nuts, grains, seeds and beans make the meal taste more alive and add a higher nutritional value. As my book suggests, nutritionally rich recipes, that are great for keeping your gut healthy, I suggest you do some research about sprouting, and the benefits of eating raw, vibrant and colorful mixings. Sprouting at home is time consuming, I tried to do it, but as a chef I buy pre sprouted. However, if you have children who are interested in this process, sprouting is both beneficial and fun. For my bowls I use sprouted adzuki beans or mung beans, the brand I buy is Tru Roots. It is simple to use, just heat the sprouts in water for 10 minutes, turn off the burner, leave the lid on and you have instantly sprouted beans.

Fermenting

Fermented veggies are delicious. But more importantly they are so important for gut health. The research about keeping our guts healthy keeps expanding with more knowledge from scientists. My favorites are beets, onions and red cabbage. As a chef I cheat and buy pre-fermented vegetables. But for families with kids fermenting can be a fun activity. I buy the glass jars of fermented veggies from the fridge section in Whole Foods. Generally found near the tofu and dairy area. Always check the brands they are stocking aren't fermented with sugar, and try to buy products as local as possible. In New York I buy the Hawthorne Valley or Real Pickles brands.

A SUPER FOOD DESERT

I love eating this combination for a desert or a snack. My book contains no deserts or appetizers as this book is about healthy, nutritious home cooked dinners. But I wanted to include this combination because it is great for kids or even for a dinner party, if you want to keep the desert healthy.

Raspberries
Chopped mint
Cacao nibs
Tahini

HOW TO MAKE IT

Place washed raspberries on a plate. Lightly drizzle tahini on top. Then add chopped mint and a few cacao nibs. A deliciously healthy and flavor-filled combination.

HEALTHY SNACKS

It has become too easy to give kids unhealthy snacks when they get home from school. Snacks are a perfect time to get Omega 3's into their growing bodies. We now know healthy fats help us all to grow stronger and keep healthy. I have also discovered children love sugary snacks in the late afternoon and then don't eat their dinner. By keeping the snacks healthier, it doesn't matter if evening meals are smaller. Here is a platter I like to throw together when kids return from school:

Mashed sardines with vinegar & vegenaise
Or mashed tinned wild salmon with vegenaise and red onion
Healthy grainy crackers
Sliced cucumbers
Seaweed strips
Avocado
Cherry tomatoes
Pumpkin seeds

FRIDGE FILLINGS MADE SIMPLE

Busy friends ask me how they can prepare meals for their family on a Sunday for the week. It seems to be an ongoing complaint of working Mums coming home from work tired, with hungry kids and not being prepared for healthy meal options. These tired, stressed moms end up grabbing easy, processed meals, or ordering in from local restaurants. My book aims to help Mums overcome this with instructions on how to fill the fridge by planning ahead. My fresh, home cooked, 3 day meal service is extremely popular both in Los Angeles and New York. Especially with larger families who have kids running in different directions.

Before heading out to the store, I come up with a 3 day meal plan, which includes 1 fish entrée, 1 meat entrée and 1 vegan entree or a different meat choice. The meals are eaten in that order. Once the menu has been decided I put together a grocery list and head out shopping. My side dishes are usually decided upon once I am in the store. Being a visual person, I shop for the veggies that are either on sale, locally produced and in season. With a well-stocked pantry at home, I come home and add toppings and dressings to my discoveries in the store.

The next step is to prep and cook all 3 meals at once. Sometimes my proteins are fully cooked before hand or left raw in a roasting pan ready to put in the oven. Same with veggies, I cut and wash them ready to use. My preferred storage containers are different sized and shaped Pyrex glass bowls and baking dishes, they come with plastic lids. During the fridge filling process I prepare one of my salads that can be taken out and eaten at any time. These salads keep nicely for 3 days. If you only mix the ingredients together as needed.

With this pre- made plan you will definitely eat healthier. I promise you.

BOWLS

The latest nutritious and delicious food craze is eating one-bowl meals. I am a huge fan of this eating style. The deliciously tasty combination of ingredients provide a varied amount of nutrients for both the body and mind. The prospect of serving bowl meals may seem overwhelming because of the number of different ingredients to prepare. By keeping the production of varied ingredients simple, this will lessen the prep time. Preparing some ingredients before hand will be useful and less time consuming, for example keeping chopped nuts and garlic mixture in the fridge for toppings at a moment's notice, sprouting beans and sauces. All prepped and ready to go. Here are a list of categories I generally provide in a bowl meal:

1. A vegetable – for example baked sweet potato, brussel sprouts, cauliflower
2. A legume – for example black beans, sprouted mung beans, black-eyed peas
3. A grain – for example quinoa, rice, millet
4. A raw green – for example kale, lettuce
5. A protein – for example fish, meat, tofu
6. A sauce – for example tahini dressing, pesto dressing
7. A fermented vegetable- for example cabbage, carrots, radishes
8. Toppings – chopped herbs, chopped nuts with garlic & nutritional yeast, nuts, seeds

For serving: place all the ingredients into one large serving bowl, with toppings and dressings in separate side bowls. Place the large serving bowl and side bowls onto the dinner table and allow guests or families serve themselves the amount they want from the serving bowl into their individual bowl. Adults and kids love this new approach to dining.

CONCLUSION

I hope my readers will enjoy feeling energized by this new approach to dining. My book has been kept simple with ingredients repeating themselves. These healthy, eating options will satisfy your kids and friends palates and the colorful plates offer up new dining options. We live in a world where all these ingredients are easily accessible to us all. Let's take advantage of this and leave behind our unhealthy habits of sugar, wheat and dairy as much as possible. Well at least eliminating from our homes. I know this to be unrealistic in most homes, and I am not against naughty snacks. But in an ideal world our kids and friends will find these flavors more appealing.

Made in United States
North Haven, CT
21 May 2024

52747943R00044